emotions

N.A. Cheatham

KEEN VISION
PUBLISHING

Printed in the United States of America

Keen Vision Publishing, LLC

www.publishwithkvp.com

ISBN: 979-8-9927392-7-5

Thank you to my friends and family who walked with me through one of the most challenging seasons of my life. Thank you for your support and prayers.

the emotions palette

amour & bonheur

(love & happiness)

A song plays in the background as I'm holding her tight
I lean in closer, hoping simple words will grab her attention
The words "thank you" softly leave my lips
A smile follows as the rhythm of our heartbeats intertwine

She slowly asks, "For what?"
The song begins to end, I simply tell her to follow the leader
A simple trail soon ends outside with no one to interfere
Where the truth that I buried deep within begins to emerge

Everything comes out, my hidden feelings reach the surface
Letting her get closer to my heart, closer than anyone has ever been
She deserves my heart along with everything else
That the rest of my life should be spent with the woman who holds it tightly

Her jaw drops as she attempts a response, she slowly picks it up with a smile
Tears of joyfulness journey down her cheeks
Leaning over to gently wipe them, I ask, "Why the tears?"
"You don't know how long I've waited to hear that," she replies, holding me tightly

dear mama

One day isn't enough to express the love a child has for their mother
She has made countless sacrifices for her children
Many sacrifices we have no knowledge of
She is always one of the biggest supporters and providers
From all of the great memories to the sad memories
A mother will show just how strong she truly is no matter the situation
Situations like raising her children while being a single mother
Over the years showing just how strong an independent woman can be
Being in school, working, and providing for her children
One day, it finally pays off as her children graduate from college
No matter the experiences each mother goes through for their children
The resilience in each one is extremely high for the sake of their children's wellbeing
With a bright smile that shines like a lighthouse
One is forever grateful for the chance to even say, "Love you, mom!"

the true meaning of love

Love is one of the strongest words someone can have in their vocabulary
If used by the wrong person, mind games can trick someone's heart severely
A word so potent it causes the bodies of true lovers to illuminate their surroundings
From the first moment of nervousness based upon the other's unknown thoughts
To the awkwardness of words that flow out of the mouth in order to impress
That is what one considers true love between those who love may last a lifetime
From trying to spend time with one another to knowing each other thoroughly
To wanting to be around each other as time itself prepares to watch the fireworks
True love is such a rare, unique connection that many people can't experience
A love that's truly strong based off of the glow and spark that blossom into a forever

cupid's target

I watch her come down the steps, and a door closes behind her
I search to understand what I have done to deserve this opportunity
To have someone as rare as her by my side, I'm within a fairytale
Where Cupid constantly shot his arrows in one direction, my heart as his target
Giving hopes of finally finding someone worth falling for without any landing
Taking a simple risk led to us conversing frequently
The past stays in the back of my mind, a past without her that I don't care to revisit
Keeping the happiness within her eyes is the only thought running circles through my mind

ella

At first glance, a beauty hypnotized them with all the sauce in her bag

Or did the consuming inhalation of leaves, some poison finally catch up to the body?

No matter the reason, there was no explanation for how she flaunted through the room

Avoiding the shackles of regret, choosing to initiate conversation, even if rejection followed

Glossing through a selection of wordplay searching for something as sharp as one's penmanship to follow, "Hey"

As if to perform a haiku to the heart standing before them

Hoping to go from enjoying each other's company to becoming each other's soulmate, one's ears wait for a response

The night is soon filled with smiles and laughs from two who started to warm up to one another

A ring catches one's attention, and they step away to address the sudden disturbance

Just to come back to an empty space, the woman who put one in a deep trance missing

Without a trace, no scent from her flowed through the air

The only thing left to hold onto is the imprint she left on one's mind

Along with a sweet name that will stay dormant within the mind, reminding one of a movie

the signs of love

At what point during your life did the thought of joy appear?
A happiness that consisted of the moment you were in love
Was it during the first encounter when words were exchanged
Where the tongue became numb, and blushing was obvious
As she laughed at the sight of nervousness and cuteness
Or the continuous conversations being held while being intrigued
By the similarities shared that drew you in deeper every second
Along with a show of fireworks being displayed just from a spark
Causing the thought of drawing them closer just to become one

Was it the personality of this person that gave off signals
Of something so rare that you didn't want to lose
Or was it the uniqueness of the similarities shared
As some may try to figure out the secret in this connection
Just to discover the difference between this person and others

Like the excitement of a child when they get their first bike
Or someone who has finally found their joy that was once lost
Knowing that this person who you just met and conversed with
May be the person who you see yourself growing old with

Who knows what journeys may open up during your path of life
As long as you are facing them together and next to one another
Nothing shall be able to shatter a bond created from beauty
A beauty so strong that it flows through the signs of love
A variety of slow jams played throughout the background
While in an uncommon place to get a fresh start on life

a siren known as hope

A soft and pleasant melody began to ring in one's eardrum
Like a siren reaching out to a lonely soul that was near

Searching for something that could be considered a safe haven
Such a place that life itself seemed to be a paradise on earth
Curiosity traveled throughout the mind as she revealed herself
Along with a voice that slowly uttered the words: "Help me."

Drawing me closer as she stood along a wall surrounded by peers
Looking as if she needed someone to rescue her from trouble
Trouble that consisted of daily struggles in a form called Life
Or just to have someone cherish her deeply by words and actions

As songs continued to play and the night started to wind down
Shyness and uncertainty were pushed to the side as courage manifested
With seconds feeling like an eternity, along with every step taken
Toward the siren called Hope as she asked, "What took so long?"

feels: the confession

Damn, why you put me on the spot like this in front of our peers
Throwing me out on stage as the limelight hits
I muster every word and emotion that laid dormant
About the woman who stands in front of me, clueless
Without a care of which route the results may go
As long as she knows she deserves the world
Whether it's from me or another, but I would rather it be me
Damn, there she goes having me choke up at a time like this
Watching me struggle with admitting the truth
That I've had my eyes on her for a while
I put clues out that led straight to my heart
While enjoying every moment of her company
Seeing and making a smile appear every chance I had
Still can't believe you have me pouring my soul out
But as the confession of my feelings comes to an end
The real question is, what will you do with this information?

drunken nights

Along with this ecstatic breeze and deadly liquid in this cup
The thought of her continues to play tug of war in my conscious
Wanting to risk everything just to hold her tightly in my arms
Needing "my issue" with her while disregarding any past flings
Knowing no other woman will match up to her diligent touch
Just to live in the moment while finishing the night with her by my side

love frequency

With this frequent vibe that flows between the two of us
Just having her company causes my mind to brainstorm
A current image of a masterpiece as if it was from one of the greatest writers
By using just my pen and paper to paint an image of her
Something far greater than the classic tale of Romeo and Juliet
A love story that doesn't pin two families against another
Instead showcases a blissful chemistry between two individuals whose bond is inseparable

what is love

"What is love?", a million-dollar question
Is it when one does for another without reward
Or when one surveys another for protection?
In reality, love is a beautiful masterpiece of emotions
One knows when love is knocking at one's doorstep
When "butterflies" or "goosebumps" take over the body
Or constant thoughts from each other daily take over the mind
The word "uncertainty" never shows its face, as it has no home
In a world that's created from each other by this word called "love"

a bright future

I was asked about how I view this term called love
Is it described as simple as a response from a flare in the sky for rescue
Coming from wherever I may be to become her Clark Kent
Just for her to know that she's my precious Lois Lane
Without a doubt, I will always come to her side whenever she is in distress
Though plenty of warnings were issued from concerning parties
Based on the type of man I was groomed into in today's brutal world
Though that's the least of the concerns that linger in our minds
Seeing each other in our most vulnerable moments
The scope of our minds became clear of a bright future along a sandy beach
I will spend the rest of this road trip down the path called infinity
With my best friend, my wife, my queen, and my soul
Just to see that smile along with a laugh of pure happiness

best friend for life

I was always told that words have to match actions
Something that's worth going into a battle headfirst
Where the reward is in the form of a woman who at first was a friend
A friend who was around through all the hardships experienced
One that was there when I needed cushion to rest my weary head
From taking on the earthquake of events to find a solution
The longer we were around one another, the closer our bond became
No one could go anywhere without seeing us together
Creating vibes that spread like a virus affecting those around
Who would have thought that she brought out this feeling
A feeling I never wanted to fumble, which meant losing her
I believe I have truly found my best friend for life

mar. 25th

As one takes to the stage to address a crowd while painting an image with just words
One cannot help but gravitate their attention towards the beautiful brown eyes in the back
While the art show of words begins to take place, one cannot help but wonder if she'll catch it
It being a hidden message to her to make up for the mishap of a proper introduction
A message that truly displays the butterflies that swelled up within the stomach
While hoping that with every brush of the color "Wordplay" caught her attention
Which would make her grow a desire for a better view of an artist in their element
As well as catching a glimpse of the pure heart that lies within one's body that could be hers
Though by the end of the finishing touches one verbally displayed and deemed as a masterpiece
Enthusiasm fills the room, but deep within the cheers, the owner of the eyes is missing
The butterflies that reside in one's stomach begin to flutter away slowly
Losing hope for the mutual butterflies of a person whose company one desires the most

e(vol)ve

Despite the amount of rollercoasters we put each other through
We always find ourselves back at each other's doorstep for one more touch
Is this what people call love?
We utter what we want to hear as our eyes connect
Without stating, we are both mesmerized by the other's body language
Hypnotizing each other as keywords are whispered
Reeling our hearts into the moment that lies in front of us as we draw closer
Causing a conflict to occur, we don't want to admit the truth
Though neither can wait until the other speaks their hidden feelings
We remain intrigued, always wanting to stay together longer in these moments

love is like the seasons

When we first met
You seemed sweet and calm
Like the spring

As we began to know each other
A warm and pleasant vibe blossomed
Like the summer

The more time we spent together
Our chemistry started to fade away
Like the fall

As things started to fall apart
Our essence became cold and bitter
Like the winter

We were once compatible
The more we spent together
Trust started to become an issue

But the more we were apart
The harder it was to function
Without the other

Causing us to rekindle
Our relationship and putting
Aside the lingering issues

Not realizing that our love
Is like the seasons of the year
They are in a cycle
That will always repeat

tristesse (sadness)

The thought of her leaving crossed my mind once
But I didn't put up a struggle for something created over the years
The fight for us has survived its last one-sided match
Exhausted of being in the presence of each other
Will we ever find each other again at another time to make amends
Or continue to travel down the dark, narrow path of no return
As the answer becomes clear, she asks for one favor
A favor that turns into a question that roughly starts with "Why"
Though answering sounds pleasant, in reality, it doesn't matter
We long ceased to refresh our chemistry to remove the strains of tiredness

medusa

Her energy gives off a sense of purity that one could build with
Energy that would possibly find me on a knee holding back tears
With a small box in my hand as I prepare to hear the word "Yes"
To falling for an infamous trap as she reveals her true nature

She goes by a variety of names, but "Medusa" is her main one
Medusa is known for luring one into a gaze with just a look
To where one turns into stone, causing them to become stuck
Just to be shown off as a mere trophy along with others

Causing everything one owns to be taken away just for laughs
"Was everything that led up to this moment just a joke?"
As one questions themselves just to hear nothing for a response
While having their words fall short as she searches for prey

Her beauty and features are astounding as she gets closer
To the next victim along the way in her path of lies and deceit
Beware of Medusa and her eyes, which are her deadliest weapon
She'll hit you with tricks just to make you feel wanted
Only to become her next prize in her showcase for an eternity

untitled, part 1

At times, one ponders what it would take
To shake off your imprint from the mind
Maybe a glass of sorrow will get the job done
Or perhaps the aroma of herbs will be better
But as time shows no trace of slowing down
The essence of you still lingers around
And the mind continues its cycle of uncertainty
One is facing a losing battle with no sign of victory
Just an open field of causalities called a shattered heart

modern day art

Vibes become one's voice as they form into the words that were once mute
While time itself sprints through the period known as "Us", keywords are forgotten
Our love vs. hate story eventually becomes another exhibit within a museum
Displaying the adventurous rollercoaster of emotions throughout our time together
Showcasing different events that led to the climax of our story before it even began
Creating a classic within the art world that depicts the inner struggles of both parties

50/50

While being in the middle of a bizarre war between desire and heartache
I find myself in a tough spot, having to make a difficult choice
Where the reward is the heart of a lovely queen that's been waiting for her "true king"
Though, I question if this situation we are in is real or fake
She knows exactly where my mind goes while being around her
Giving off the same wavelength that's synced to the rhythm of my heartbeat
No amount of words or anybody can break this unique link
Even though she's off the market, and we're not supposed to cross that line
Seeing her face along with that gaze and smile can make one break their oath
An oath to never revert to their old ways as the desire for her touch
Along with her love still lingers in every corner of the heart and mind

in too deep

Most days, we go through this unique routine
Calling about having a moment of loneliness
Just to end up at her residence to be used
She continues to state how it's no feelings attached
But why send out this so-called "distress signal" for one's love
Knowing these precious memories will eventually build up
Causing an unexpected brutal war between the heart and mind
With the heart wanting to announce her as "sweetheart"
While the mind lives for this adventurous thrill of excitement
One comes to the thought of the easiness of venturing away
Only to come to a realization of being stuck in her web of lust
By heading towards the phone as it slowly rings endlessly

under her thumb

Still can't believe that I eventually found my match
With someone who loves to play as many games as me
As if we're on a seesaw, enjoying each other's company
Though the only difference is whenever she calls or text
I immediately stop what I'm doing just to go wherever she is
Many told me to cut all ties with her, but it always goes in one ear and out the other
She puts such a trance on me that I can't let go of her
Even if she isn't good for one's heart, mind, and soul
All defenses that surrounded the heart don't exist anymore
Due to her having complete control of the heart
This "must be love" is all but an illusion she creates based on memories
Memories which cloud the true scenery that I'm not ready to see
A portrait of me being completely trapped under her thumb

drinking you away

As I sit in this bar on a late Friday night
With you on my mind, I begin to feel ill
Just thinking about your smile and scent
I ask the bartender for another round

Three cups in, and you continue to pop up
As I am steadily reminded of our happiness
Together and also of the pain we caused each other
Two more cups should make these memories vanish

Now it's closing time, and five cups in
The thought of you begins to fade, and I'm in the clear
Though we had splendid memories together
We also had heartbreaking memories as well

So as I try to gather myself before leaving
I hear a bell ring like a whistle as a door swings open
And a face too familiar brightens up the room
The same ill feeling reoccurs as we lock eyes
I ask the bartender for one more drink to go
As I walk into the night trying to drink you away

the disaster called love

As one sits in complete silence while fading into a deep conscious
With the brain roaming while trying to figure out why Cupid set us up
"Was he just playing around as he shot his arrows in multiple directions?"
Hitting a target that felt like home just for it to slowly crumble away
Just wanting to find something that's worth one's time and love
Though her toxic traits leave a bad taste in the mouth
The word "love" begins to sound more like "disaster" as this ship sinks

mental scars

Shooting side eyes in my direction all because of my nonchalant patterns
Is it my fault that I'm not an open book for everyone to have access to read
Or is it my fault that I don't converse much with you unless it involves intimacy
Maybe it's from the amount of options I have stored due to past stages of life
Just by revealing everything that I locked away deep within a dungeon far in my mind
To having it thrown into my face as if it was a piece of pie just because pettiness took over
These uncalled-for scars may have healed on the outside of my body
But the damage created a mental trauma where the access of me is faded

untitled, part 2

Someone once said that if you never speak your mind
How would you know if the response falls in your favor
So, if I'm being honest about how I feel for her
Then I'm laying it all on the line for a "heart-to-heart"
The thought of her still lingers in my mind like a scent
Though I've tried to delete her essence from the bank
All that remains is a glimpse of her beauty and frame
"Why can't I let go of something that doesn't exist?
Something that felt real but, in reality, was just for show.
Was it all for fun, or did she just want to see me vulnerable?"
As these questions continue to appear in the mind
There is one question that never comes to the surface
"Was there ever a chance for us to grow into love?"
But the heart can't bring the mind to wonder about the answer
As the shield of defense for the heart has been shattered
Causing us to fall prey to plenty of wolves in sheep's clothing
Will we bounce back from a defeat that was bound to happen
Or will we wake up to the realization of our own uncertainty?

maybe so, maybe not

You once asked me if there was still happiness in our union
With the constant disagreements and trust issues always lingering
At first glance, it wasn't even a question due to no solution
While not considering the possibility of what would be missed
Besides the downward spiral, our love was once genuine
But living in a repetitive cycle took its toll on our minds and actions
Is there a reset button on us or a white flag to give up on this pain
Should our happiness over the years be put into consideration
Or is the toxic environment called "Us" the final scene of our love

love is like the seasons, part 2

While it's in the middle of spring
The memories of her began to flourish
Of a peaceful vibe that was once given off
And how kindhearted her personality was

Thought I had discovered something real at first
The warmth of our chemistry began to spark
Setting off flames so hot as if it was the summertime
But too blinded by love to see the early signs

As time continued to move while being a unit
Our chemistry began to deteriorate drastically
Due to a once solid trust which started to fade away
Quick, like our love was the color of leaves in the fall

Her aroma appeared to go down a dark, cold path
Creating plenty of distance and less talking between us
Much time was wasted while putting forth the effort
To conquer this new chill never seen before in the winter

uncertainty

"Does she feel the same way that I do?"
"Did I give myself away by saying too much?"
These are just a few questions that always pop up

As I give my best efforts to win her attention
Through all of the timely conversations
While painting all of the clues onto a canvas
Did she notice the portrait of my feelings?
Or did she not notice my heart blended in the paint?

Not knowing someone's exact thoughts and feelings
About you or anyone else they come in contact with
Is one of the worst headaches in the world that hurts to the core
Because their reactions toward you are out of your control

So, should I continue to follow her blindly down this path
A path that's narrow and leads into a dark and unknown abyss?
Or should I begin to explore the horizon with multiple options
Who show signs of wanting to become my soulmate?

Even though I'm not within the party of forfeiters
Nor the type to become a juggler with multiple options at leisure
But I'm the type that is ready to become her knight in shining armor
While she instantly becomes my main focus throughout life
Just to be by her side during the highs and lows
Just to know her exact terrors and heartaches

Just to watch her blossom into the world day by day
Just to be glad to call her my everlasting wife

But while I constantly daydream about a future with her
As if being with her begins to feel like every day is a reset
I gradually start to come to a realization that she is like time itself
And I am put into a prism of torture that involves an infinity of uncertainty

colère & dépression (anger & depression)

As she storms towards me with a raging voice that makes the walls cry
The mind wanders off to form the question of how we arrived here
At this moment, where the possibility of a return to the beginning seems low
Where a love so strong at the start of our union now is crumbling slowly

The mind starts to ease back into the reality of the screams and echoes
All over what outsiders say just to watch our Rome burn during the night
While the useless feeling of an opinion circulates throughout the body
Her actions prove the side she chose as the slander continues to be thrown

Defeat is inevitable, with jealousy being the key factor from the outsiders
With cherished memories becoming tarnished as the arguing continues
Soon, the lose-lose battle is over, and the constant yelling becomes quiet
All that is left in the end is the tears from her as she lays by herself

haunting melody

As the moon slowly begins to come out within the night
One tries to prepare for a pleasant slumber in order to reset
Though, as soon as the eyes meet a place called "the dark void"
The face of a woman from the past lingers through the darkness
Deciding to play games with one's mind just for the thrill of it
As she has the heart entangled in strings while playing different notes
With each one replaying haunting memories we don't want to remember
Causing one to want to continue attending her musical
"Will I ever break this so-called curse she has on the heart?
Or will I continue to have these battles within the night?"

2am on I-10

Why did the morning transition into the night without any warnings
Probably since the mind has been a little clouded from daily obstacles
The brain sends signals to the fingers as one shoots a risky shot
Considering if I should've reached out to a love, even if it comes off a little selfish
As I fiend for her touch, her support, and her presence just to live in the moment
Knowing deep within her heart, I lie dormant since we share the same desires
Though our pride and ego continue to be stubborn about admitting the truth
But with just a press of a button follows a response that gives a "peace of mind"
I slide through lanes, my destination a lonely heart that needs tender loving care

forbidden

Is it selfish for one to admit that they don't want to share a woman
who is on a forbidden list?
Desiring the softness from her hands all the way to her lips
as they touch every inch of one's body
In order to provide the body with a certain healing treatment
that one's own partner lacks
Having her within reach as eyes are locked onto one another
while the bodies build a rhythm
With no regard for getting caught in the act of infidelity
since the track of time has been lost
The only thing that matters is time itself becomes an infinity
the moment she's within one's space

toxicity

It's crazy how you can't erase this word called "hate" from our vocabulary
During the times when she creates a random argument
Which usually stems from her insecurities, but she doesn't want to admit it
To think that at one point in our time together, she was called "beloved"
Now, one tries not to mix her name along with this "hate" word
Just for her to become a sour patch kid once she's feeling bad
From her continuing to start these confrontations just for fun
Or is it really because one doesn't partake in her toxic ways
So ready to end this "seesaw" of a relationship
Can't even retain the good memories that are clouded by her habits

really

Don't know why she's expecting anyone to play this back-and-forth "game" with her
While knowing all it takes is for me to dial a number from within a book titled "GTD"
Just to dismiss her from the obligations of being my partner in crime
As I prepare to continue moving forward without any memories of us
While another's face replaces the one that seemed familiar but stayed in the rearview mirror

split personality

With every step I take throughout life,
along with the air that fills the lungs with each inhale
A little birdie tries her best to tag along for a ride
without knowing we're at an amusement park
Thinking that she's my passenger princess
just to be unaware of which number she pulled
Words are uttered just to wrap her heart within strings
while my fingers conduct an orchestra
Just to enjoy every second with her until our timeframe expires
as it resets for who's next
Falling asleep with a different face by my side every night
feels like a pleasant and fun dream
Only to become a nightmare as I glance into a mirror every morning, puzzled
By her version of Hyde staring back at me without knowing
if Jekyll was really in charge

secretly drowning

Should one be ashamed of admitting that we want her company
That we need her in our presence, our space, and our hands
As being around her daily causes us to fall deeper and deeper for her
Even if she already has someone by her side that causes issues
Being ready to intervene for the sake of making her a true queen
While knowing that once we revert back to our old ways
There will be no going back, as she is truly worth every consequence
But in reality, the biggest fear is within oneself as we are unaware
Uncertain about her true feelings that she has about us
Knowing that we are framed as a portrait within the chamber deep in her mind
As these mutual butterflies flutter around every time our paths cross
Is she really ready to step away from her current situation
And start anew with someone who doesn't come with uncertainty
Or willing to work out all of the kinks in her armor from her union
Whichever pill one decides to digest and prepare for the outcome of
One may be able to sleep comfortably at night next to their puppeteer
Or suffer from a sudden shock as they try to repair their heart
From a tragic heartbreak that one will not be able to recover from

hypnotized

After the amount of time spent together with her
She still tries to hide her true feelings towards me
Even though the writing is on the wall for how deep in love she is
For the person who created a certain atmosphere in which she craves for
The thought of building a foundation with her continues to sprout in the mind
But within this fantasy that dwells in the mind constantly
The everlasting back and forth about trust issues of infidelity appears
"Maybe I should cheat."
"Maybe I should creep."
The mind eventually wanders off on its own journey with no destination
With a constant reminder of her toxic traits but also the thrill from them
Just to realize my love from the excitement that comes from these arguments
That both of us knowing the other isn't escaping this torture
Of being accused of breaking an oath every single day
Without realizing that we're hypnotized by something called a "toxic love"

two sides of a street

It's funny how one came to the conclusion that she was right
About our toxic situation with both not ready to let go
Of each other for something that's waiting for us, which is better
Though at the moment where one sees the other taking steps forward
Those steps shortly retrace back to their roots as a reset button is pressed
With a simple "I miss you" text being sent out bringing up the past
A past where, besides the negatives, there were more positives that were clouded
Then, the recollection of memories of all the long nights swells up in the head
Soon to find the other instantly at one's doorstep, stating how it's the last time
That she will be within our grasp where one doesn't care about the next person
With being more fixated on her soft creamy skin flowing freely through the hands
Of someone who enjoys this toxicity where saying one thing actually means another
When, in reality, one doesn't see a future with her but enjoys this so-called "fun time"
Orchestrating the perfect symphony while being the conductor of her heart
As her happiness eventually shows how one isn't ready to branch away from her

vultures

As soon as the silent moon brightens the dark sky
Plenty of lonely vultures begin to take flight
On the prowl while searching for a quick meal
As they crowd the cellular of one for a response
Just to become disappointed from being ignored
Off of the first glance, as one's time is occupied
Though, at times, these options are appealing
Mainly from verbal struggles between parties
Feeling like roadkill just from the arguments
Soon, the vultures take notice of what's left
To start swarming a heart whose soul has faded

to my fallen brother

Looking back on the countless talks we would always have
Mainly about random stuff that would turn into hours passing by
Or even when we spent most of the time socializing with our brotherhood
Not one day goes by without thinking about not being able to speak with my brother
anymore
From growing up with someone who was a key figure in shaping many lives
To being a true friend that anyone could talk to without being judged
As he illuminated every person's life he crossed paths with
Just to not be coming back one day based on a news reporting
Even though years have passed by since you were taken from us violently
It still feels as if it was just yesterday that the details were told
Though you still shine deep within everyone's heart and mind
Watching us accomplish feats we once talked about as if it were yesterday
Knowing that you would want us to continue to push forward while giving us strength
It was an honor to have been able to call you a true brother, Darius Johnson

false reality

Ever get asked, "How's everything been so far?"
While thinking of only the positives that stand out
As all the negatives that one has encountered stared back
With a diabolical smile that gave off a sense of jealousy
"Go ahead and tell them the truth. A truth that consists of pain."
A pain that sinks all the way to the core of one's own body
Whether from abuse in all forms or even mental blocks from a terror
Soon to take over the body like a virus without any signs of a cure

thoughts called nightmares

Nights like this one always drift away at their own pace
Eventually into a vague nightmare filled with horrors
Which consists of drowning in one's own pain
As one sinks away slowly within a quicksand of thoughts
No amount of resistance to clear the mind seems to be helping
One is pulled deeper and deeper into an abyss
With no signs of a clear path for escaping the depths of one's mind

art of violence

In today's society, it's pretty common to see a straight bloodbath on tv
With mass shootings in public settings, including schools
And even our quiet neighborhoods where people of the same background and ethnicity live
Brainstorm blueprints to eliminate one another just for a senseless reason
Reasons that may vary between women, bragging rights, egos, religions, or even just because
It's as if we're in an era where violence seems to be the main language we speak
As other languages become obsolete due to the lack of simply talking to one another about our feelings
To find common ground with one another to have a better understanding of our backgrounds and beliefs
Leaving any judgmental thoughts in the mental
Though, in reality, hatred slowly forms within one's heart
Flowing through the bloodstream, causing one to act on their own free will to perform an art of violence

dear nile

Do you remember the first time our paths crossed?
Where an "Excuse me miss. You dropped something,"
Led to years of fun with the one person who felt like a dream come true
Just to one day become sour, losing sweetness
The thought of continuing this life's journey with the one person I loved
Crushed every emotion that lingered in this body that was once yours
From loving, playful happiness and confidence in this person
Just to fade into sadness, anger, scariness, and embarrassment
This so-called "world" I envisioned with my partner-in-crime for eternity
Soon crumbled away at its own pace, me trying to pick up the pieces
The person I've become wants to wish you nothing but the best
While the person who was tormented for years hopes karma eventually shows her face
I take this time to muster up all these swollen heartaches of torture
And jot down a rollercoaster of feelings towards the one who I saw a future with
I hope that one day you see within that empty vessel of yours
That the heart you once said we shared
Was nothing more than a fragment of empty promises from old wounds

connect with the author

N.A. Cheatham was born in Richmond, Virginia and later moved to Baton Rouge, Louisiana, where he currently resides. His interest in poetry began in high school. As he started writing more poems he became fully committed to translating thoughts onto paper to help clear his mind of everyday challenges....and the writing continues...

Here are a few ways you can connect with the author.

facebook   NILE CHEATHAM
instagram   @NILEBEEZY

www.ingramcontent.com/pod-product-compliance
Lightning Source LLC
Chambersburg PA
CBHW081158090426

42736CB00017B/3376